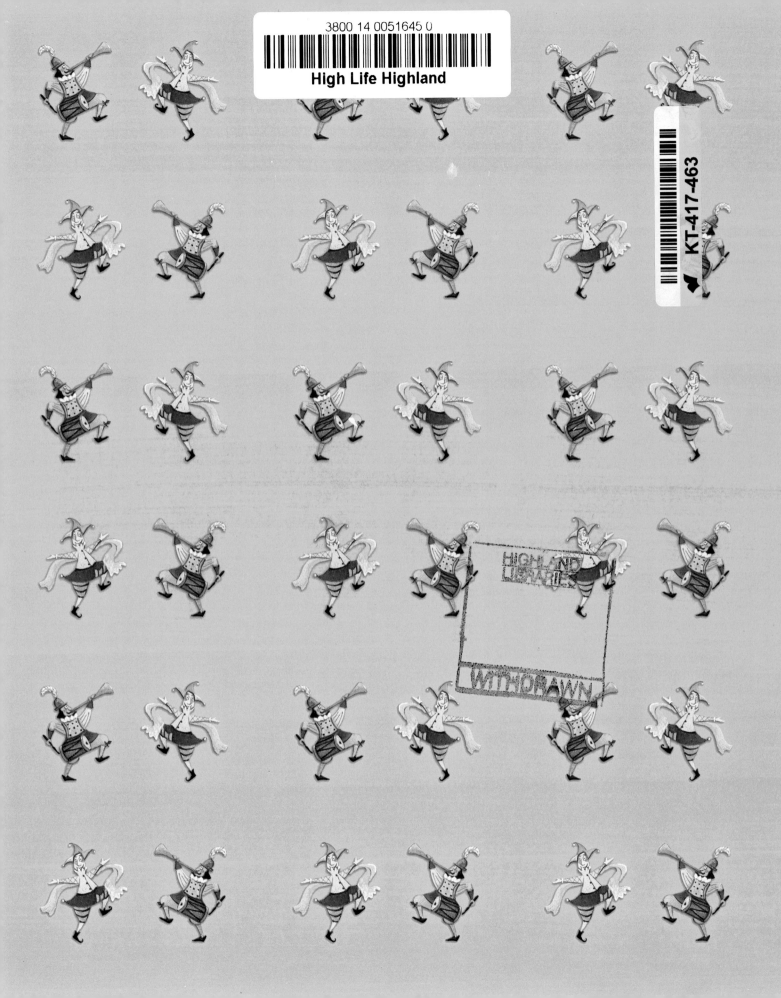

"He was a man, take him for all in all,
I shall not look upon his like again."

Hamlet

First published in 2014 by Franklin Watts
Text © Penny Worms 2014
Illustrations © Adria Meserve 2014

Franklin Watts, 338 Euston Road, London NW1 3BH
Franklin Watts Australia, Level 17/207 Kent Street, Sydney, NSW 2000

Produced by Penny Worms & Graham Rich, Book Packagers.
Typeset in Parma Petit and Minion Pro. Cover type aka Potsley.
With special thanks to Tim Knapman for his ideas and enthusiasm at the start of this project,
and to Anna Claybourne for her own special writing gift.

A CIP catalogue record for this book is available from the British Library.

ISBN 978 1 4451 3187 0
Library eBook ISBN 978 1 4451 4237 1
Printed in China

Franklin Watts is a division of Hachette Children's Books, an Hachette UK company.

www.hachette.co.uk

The Comedy, History & Tragedy of

William Shakespeare

Adria Meserve

written by Anna Claybourne

with Timothy Knapman

FRANKLIN WATTS

LONDON • SYDNEY

Contents

The Seven Ages of *William Shakespeare*

". . . One man in his time plays many parts, his Acts being Seven Ages . . ."

1. The Infant

William Shakespeare was born in Stratford-upon-Avon on 23 April 1564. He was the first son of John Shakespeare, a glove-maker and important local citizen, and Mary, the daughter of a successful farmer. Neither parent could read nor write.

2. The Schoolboy

Because his father was an alderman (a local councillor), Shakespeare had a free education at the King Edward VI Grammar School in Stratford.

3. The Lover

At the age of 18, Shakespeare married Anne Hathaway, who was eight years older and pregnant with their first daughter, Susanna. It's not known if they married for love or because they had to, but they spent a lot of their lives apart. Their twins, Hamnet and Judith, were born in 1585, but Hamnet died tragically when he was just 11.

4. The Lost Years

What Shakespeare did in the seven years between 1585 and 1592 is a mystery. Perhaps he became a tutor or went to fight overseas. But by 1592, we know he was in London, beginning to find fame as a playwright and actor.

5. The Success

Over 20 years, Shakespeare wrote or co-wrote over 38 plays. His poem *Venus and Adonis*, written in 1593, was a bestseller for years. He was part-owner of an acting company and two theatres. He became a rich man.

6. The Homecoming

Shakespeare bought New Place, a large house in Stratford, for his family in 1597. By the early 1610s, Shakespeare was spending most of his time there. He stopped writing plays and lived the life of a rich landowner. He died in April 1616, on or around his 52nd birthday.

7. The Afterlife

Shakespeare doesn't seem to have been interested in what happened to his plays after his death. It was two actors from his company who, in 1623, first thought to produce the *First Folio*, a printed work that included most of his plays. As the years passed, Shakespeare's fame grew and he is now celebrated as one of the greatest writers who ever lived.

Stratford-upon-Avon, 1564

Stratford-upon-Avon was a busy countryside town in central England. Though it wasn't a big city, it was a centre for the local area. There were ironmongers, butchers, cobblers and tailors, as well as inns, churches, and a local council, just like the ones towns have today. Farmers and traders would gather there on market days. Travelling musicians and theatre troupes would visit the town – their shows may have inspired the young Shakespeare!

Holy Trinity Church

Travelling performers

Market Square

Henley Street

Records from the Holy Trinity Church, Stratford's main church, show that Shakespeare was baptised there on 26 April 1564. His father, John, owned several houses in the town, but it's thought that Will was born in this one, on Henley Street. The large, three-storey Tudor house still stands today, and is now the Shakespeare's Birthplace Trust Museum. You can visit it and look around the rooms and hallways where Shakespeare grew up.

John Shakespeare

Shakespeare's father was a successful maker of gloves and leather goods. Over time, he became an important person in Stratford. He was on the town council, and became Stratford's mayor in 1568.

Mary Arden

Shakespeare's mother was the daughter of a well-off farmer. When John Shakespeare lost a lot of his money in the 1570s, it was his wife's wealth that came to the rescue.

The Black Death

Will was John and Mary's third child. Their first two children, Joan and Margaret, had died as babies, which was common in those days. Elizabethan England suffered terribly from bubonic plague, or the Black Death. This was a deadly disease spread by fleas living on rats. One outbreak hit Stratford in July 1564, so Will was lucky to survive.

JOAN
SHAKESPEARE
DIED 1558
AGED 2 MONTHS

MARGARET
SHAKESPEARE
DIED 1562
AGED 1 YEAR

Shakespeare's World

Shakespeare was born into one of the most powerful countries in the world, at one of the most exciting times in history. While he was growing up, Queen Elizabeth I was on the throne. She ruled over an age of amazing art, culture, science and exploration. Yet it was also a time of war and power struggles. Elizabeth often had to fight off deadly enemies. All of this must have affected Shakespeare and influenced his works.

The Renaissance

Europe was going through a time known as the Renaissance, which means "rebirth". The methods of the ancient Greeks and Romans became fashionable again. Architects copied their buildings and writers revived their writing styles. Shakespeare often borrowed characters and stories from ancient Greek and Roman legends and history books.

Exploration

It was also the great age of exploration. Explorers from Europe had discovered the Americas, the "New World", and made the first ever round-the-world sailing trip. They brought back valuable treasures and exotic discoveries, such as pineapples and chocolate. They told tales of adventure, unexplored lands, strange animals and unknown peoples.

Art and Invention

It was a time of great creativity, when artists, musicians and writers produced exciting new works. Inventions appeared, such as the telescope and printing press. Old beliefs were replaced with fresh ideas – people began to accept that the Earth was round and not flat, and that it revolved around the Sun, instead of being in the centre of the Universe.

Religion

Before Henry VIII, the main religion in England was Catholic, but Henry became a Protestant and formed the Church of England. Elizabeth was Protestant, too, and Catholics were badly treated, especially after a group of Catholic noblemen plotted against her. Shakespeare would have been aware of these religious struggles in his youth.

Queen Elizabeth I

Elizabeth was the last of the Tudor monarchs. She was the daughter of King Henry VIII and his second wife, Anne Boleyn. Elizabeth was a great leader, seeing off plots and invasions to stay on the throne for 44 years. She loved art and culture, especially theatre, and London was buzzing with life. She paid actors and and musicians to perform for her.

"We shall shortly have a famous victory!"

In 1588, when Shakespeare was 14, Spain, a Catholic country, sent a fleet of ships, known as the Spanish Armada, to invade England and overthrow Elizabeth. The Queen herself made a war speech to her armies at Tilbury, and her powerful warships and clever planning fought off the attack. This made England even more of a country to be reckoned with.

School Life: Stratford, 1568–78

In Elizabethan times, not everyone went to school. Of the boys who did, most only went between the ages of four and seven. At seven, they had to go to work to help support their families. But Shakespeare was lucky. Because his father was an important man, Will was taught up to the age of 14 at the King Edward VI Grammar School. Not that he would have felt lucky. The school day started at 6 am (7 am in the winter) and went on till 5.30 or 6 pm, six days a week. It's not surprising that Jaques, in the play *As You Like It*, talks about the "whining school-boy . . . creeping like snail unwillingly to school".

Only upper-class girls were educated; they were taught at home by private tutors. Other girls spent their days helping with the domestic chores, or learning how to become a good wife.

The Horn Book

At primary school, the pupils would learn their alphabet and the Lord's prayer from a "horn book". The printed text was covered by a see-through layer of horn and mounted onto a piece of wood shaped like a square table-tennis bat.

The boys were taught Latin, the language of ancient Rome, and the Protestant version of Christianity. There was lots of testing and learning by heart.

Shakespeare and his classmates would put on Latin plays and learn how to speak in public. Mathematics was not considered as important, so was only studied when there were spare moments in the day.

A scrivener would come in to teach the boys to write. They would use quill pens with ink. The boys brought their own quills into school every day, along with their notebooks and a candle for when it got dark.

The worst day for the boys would have been Friday. Besides revisions and tests of the week's work, the teacher handed out punishments for any misbehaviour during the week. It was common for teachers to beat or whip children with a birch cane for swearing, fighting or talking in English when they should have been talking in Latin.

The boys were taught how to turn prose into verse, copy the writing styles of different authors, and retell old stories so they seemed fresh and exciting. All these skills would prove very useful to Shakespeare when he came to write his own plays.

London, 1592

Like many ambitious young men, Shakespeare travelled to London to seek his fortune. It was the only place in England where a talented writer could make his name and start a successful career. Going to the theatre was the latest fashion and it was the start of a boom time for writers and actors. But London was also filthy, smelly, crowded, noisy and dangerous!

London was one of the largest and richest cities in Europe. Trade with Europe and the Americas was thriving and ships thronged the docks.

The severed heads of noblemen found guilty of treason were stuck on spikes at the entrances to London Bridge as a terrible warning to others.

The air was badly polluted by the smoke from brick kilns, tanneries and smithies.

The city was infested with disease-ridden black rats so there were frequent outbreaks of bubonic plague. It could wipe out whole families in a matter of days.

People went just outside the city for their entertainment. Bankside was an area full of taverns, bowling alleys, wrestling rings and shooting galleries. There were also cockpits and bearpits. Bear-baiting was a savage but hugely popular pastime. Crowds cheered as wild dogs fought bears that were chained to posts.

The water was so foul that most people drank beer instead, even children!

There were no toilets so people emptied their chamberpots out of the window. The cobbled streets were slick with filth.

Shakespeare spent most of his working life in this city of violence and possibility, of pleasure and cruelty, of crowds and noise and endless bustle. Its spirit is everywhere in his plays.

17

Map of Shakespeare's London

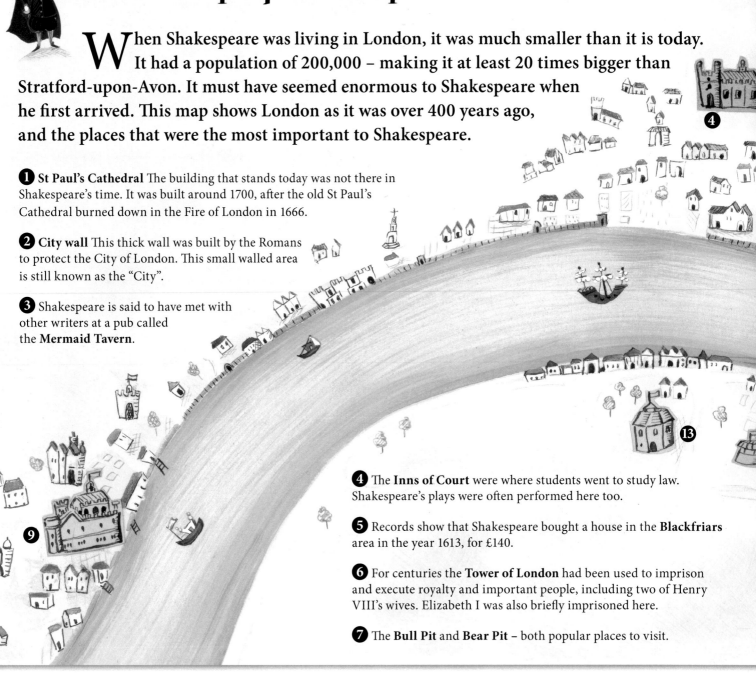

When Shakespeare was living in London, it was much smaller than it is today. It had a population of 200,000 – making it at least 20 times bigger than Stratford-upon-Avon. It must have seemed enormous to Shakespeare when he first arrived. This map shows London as it was over 400 years ago, and the places that were the most important to Shakespeare.

1 **St Paul's Cathedral** The building that stands today was not there in Shakespeare's time. It was built around 1700, after the old St Paul's Cathedral burned down in the Fire of London in 1666.

2 **City wall** This thick wall was built by the Romans to protect the City of London. This small walled area is still known as the "City".

3 Shakespeare is said to have met with other writers at a pub called the **Mermaid Tavern**.

4 The **Inns of Court** were where students went to study law. Shakespeare's plays were often performed here too.

5 Records show that Shakespeare bought a house in the **Blackfriars** area in the year 1613, for £140.

6 For centuries the **Tower of London** had been used to imprison and execute royalty and important people, including two of Henry VIII's wives. Elizabeth I was also briefly imprisoned here.

7 The **Bull Pit** and **Bear Pit** – both popular places to visit.

The Theatres

At first plays were performed in inn-yards – outdoor spaces around inns and taverns. But in 1572, public performances were banned from the City of London, to try to stop the spread of the Black Death. So people began building theatres outside the city walls.

8 The **Theatre** in Shoreditch was the first of London's proper theatres. It was built in 1576, before Shakespeare came to London. It was used by the Chamberlain's Men, the theatre company that Shakespeare joined.

9 **Whitehall Palace** Shakespeare's theatre company performed plays at this royal palace for Queen Elizabeth I, and later King James I. Most of the palace was destroyed by fire in 1698.

10 The **Curtain Theatre** sprang up in 1577, very near The Theatre in Shoreditch. Shakespeare's company played here too.

SHOREDITCH

CITY OF LONDON

BLACKFRIARS

THAMES RIVER

LONDON BRIDGE

BANKSIDE

 11 The Rose Theatre, built in 1587, was the first theatre built over the river. This area is still home to theatres and arts centres today.

 12 Blackfriars Theatre was part of an existing building bought by James Burbage, a leader of the Chamberlain's Men. In 1596, he turned it into a posh, high-class theatre. Unlike most theatres, it had a roof, so Shakespeare's company put on plays here in the winter, when it was too rainy and dark for outdoor shows.

 13 The Swan Theatre was built in 1594 close to the Rose. The Swan was one of the biggest and most popular theatres of the time.

 14 The Globe Theatre was built in 1599 by the Chamberlain's Men. This is the theatre most associated with Shakespeare and his works. It only stood until 1644, but there is now a modern Globe in the same area.

Elizabethan Theatres

In Elizabethan times, going to the theatre was a new, exciting fashion. It was a popular pastime for people from all walks of life to go and see a play – very like going to the cinema today.

Like many theatres, Shakespeare's Globe was ring-shaped. This design was copied from the open-air theatres of ancient Greece and Rome. No one knows what the Globe looked like inside exactly, but it would have looked something like this...

Lighting

As there were no stage lights, most plays were shown in the afternoon, when there was plenty of daylight. They started at around 2 or 3 pm, and ran for two or three hours.

Thatched roof

Toilets

There were no toilets – people would go outside and squat wherever suited them!

The Flag
A flag would announce the play that was being performed.

Sparky special effects!
There weren't many safety rules in those days, so actors would fire real cannons in battle scenes. In 1613, a spark from a cannon used during the play *Henry VIII* set light to the roof of the Globe, and the whole theatre burned down! Luckily, everyone escaped and the Globe was quickly rebuilt.

The Heavens – a canopy to keep the actors dry

Upper stage for balcony scenes

Musician's gallery

Seating
There were three storeys of seating, called galleries, covered with a roof. You paid up to sixpence to sit here, or in private boxes, called the gentlemen's rooms. Some people paid a penny or two extra for a comfy cushion to sit on.

Door to the tiring house, a room backstage

Trap door

Stage

Standing
It usually cost one penny to go into the standing area in front of the stage. The people who stood here were known as the "groundlings".

Going to the Theatre

If you go to the theatre today, you'll probably wear smart clothes and sit quietly during the show. Not so in Shakespeare's time! Going to the theatre was a noisy, rowdy experience. It could even be a bit scary. Theatres were rough places, where you could have your purse stolen or get pelted with a rotten egg.

Theatregoers didn't stay still or keep quiet! They chatted, munched snacks and milled about throughout the show. Snack sellers and pickpockets roamed around among the crowds.

Heckling and throwing food at the actors was commonplace. Sometimes fights broke out between audience members, too.

"Get him off!"

"That's rubbish!"

Behind the scenes

Theatres showed several plays each week, so there wasn't time to set up detailed scenery. Instead, the actors relied on costumes, props and language to set the scene.

Dramatic entrances

Trap doors above and below the stage would enable actors to make dramatic entrances. In the play *The Tempest*, for example, the spirit Ariel would appear from "The Heavens" above, and Caliban would crawl up from "Hell" below.

The tiring house

The tiring house was the room behind the stage where the actors rested and got changed for different scenes. Sometimes an actor would play different parts, so a costume change transformed him into another character.

Costumes

Normal Elizabethans couldn't wear whatever they liked. It was actually against the law for a servant to wear the clothes of a nobleman! But actors were allowed to wear lavish costumes. This made the whole theatrical experience even more exciting for the audience.

Becoming female

There were no female actors at all – the stage was not seen as a fit place for a woman. Instead, boys or young men put on high voices, wigs and make-up to play female roles. But make-up in those days contained lead, which is poisonous, and so boy actors often had skin diseases and sometimes died from lead poisoning.

Props

Props were usually small, portable things such as a skull, a shield or a flower. Daggers and swords were essential for battle scenes, and the actors had to know how to use them because they were real!

Bloody battles

Real animals' blood was used to add a touch of realism to the battle and murder scenes. Handkerchiefs and sponges were soaked in it, and sometimes a pig's bladder filled with blood was hidden underneath clothing for a really gory, dramatic effect.

King James I

The Company

The Chamberlain

In Elizabethan times, just as today, theatre companies ran theatres and put on plays. Shakespeare's company was called the Chamberlain's Men. It changed its name to the King's Men in 1603, when King James VI of Scotland succeeded Elizabeth to become King James I of Great Britain. Members of the King's Men did all sorts of jobs – some, like Shakespeare, did many.

William Shakespeare
Actor, writer and manager

Who was the Chamberlain?

The Lord Chamberlain organized entertainment for the court of Elizabeth I – especially theatre, which she loved. In 1594, when Shakespeare's theatre company was set up, the Chamberlain became the company's patron. This meant he supported the company and paid them to perform for the Queen.

James Burbage

The brains behind the company, James Burbage was a carpenter before he became an actor and businessman. After working for several theatre companies, he set up the Chamberlain's Men in 1594. He also built The Theatre, and set up the Blackfriars Theatre.

Richard Burbage

Richard Burbage, the son of James Burbage, was the company's star actor and a famous celebrity of his time. He played big lead roles such as *Macbeth*, *Hamlet* and *Othello*, and was known for his brilliant memory and beautiful voice.

Cuthbert Burbage

Richard's brother Cuthbert was in the company too, but was involved in theatre-building rather than acting.

William Kempe

A famous clown, dancer and actor, Will Kempe often played comedy roles, such as Bottom in *A Midsummer Night's Dream*. He was known for his on-stage jigs, and once danced all the way from London to Norwich – nine days of dancing!

Robert Armin

When Kempe left the company in 1599, Robert Armin took over as the comedy star. Because of him, the fool or clown became more detailed, clever and central to the play – as seen in Shakespeare's later plays, such as *King Lear.*

Augustine Phillips

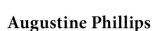

Phillips was a wealthy celebrity who was with the company for many years. He may have played the parts of older men, such as Prospero in *The Tempest* and as Jaques in *As You Like It.* He was also a musician, and probably played (and maybe even wrote) the music for the songs in Shakespeare's plays.

Henry Condell and John Heminges

Condell and Heminges were actors in the company as well as Shakespeare's friends. They are most famous for collecting his plays after his death, and publishing a collection of them in the *First Folio* in 1623.

Boy actors

Younger boy actors were hired to play the female roles. Some of them later became company members, too.

Extras

The company would hire extra actors to play the smaller parts. If they did well, they might eventually join the company as full members.

Shakespeare's Craft

In the 1500s, few people could write at all. It is thought that only 20 per cent of men and 5 per cent of women could sign their own name. Shakespeare's mother couldn't write, though she came from a wealthy family. She drew a picture of a horse as her signature. Those who did learn to write were mainly the wealthy and those involved in the church.

Shakespeare's stories

Shakespeare is famous for his tales of wild adventures, passionate lovers, jealous murderers, kings, queens and power struggles. However, he rarely made up the stories he told in his plays. Instead, he borrowed existing stories from myths, legends, other writers and history books. It was the way he wove these stories together and used language to create vivid characters and dramatic scenes that make his plays so memorable.

Shakespeare's style

Shakespeare was brilliant at writing lyrical, beautiful and moving descriptions and speeches. He was very skilled with poetic techniques and used a mixture of styles – blank verse, prose, poetry and song.

Blank verse is a regular, rhythmic pattern of words, with five beats or stresses in every line. Here are some examples from Romeo and Juliet.

Writing tools

Shakespeare wrote all his plays by hand on paper. He probably used a quill pen made from a goose feather, dipped into ink. Writers would use two or more quill pens at a time, writing with one and leaving another in the ink ready to use. Shakespeare also needed plenty of candles to write by during the hours of darkness.

ROMEO: But soft! What light through yonder window breaks?
It is the east, and Juliet is the sun...

This is a metaphor, comparing Juliet's beauty to the bright light of the Sun, by saying that she IS the sun.

JULIET: My bounty is as boundless as the sea,
My love as deep. The more I give to thee,
The more I have, for both are infinite...

Juliet uses similes, comparing her feelings of love to the vast sea.

JULIET: Good night, good night!
Parting is such sweet sorrow
That I shall say good night till it be morrow.

Blank verse mostly doesn't rhyme, but sometimes the last two lines in a scene do rhyme, to round things off nicely.

Here are some words whose first appearance is in a Shakespeare work. And if Shakespeare didn't know of a word he wanted, he made one up!

blanket
bloodstained
blushing
cold-hearted
eyeball
gloomy
gossip
laughable
luggage
moonbeam
silliness
torture

Prose is normal language, with no particular patterns or rhymes. Shakespeare often uses prose for comic scenes and the speech of working-class characters. Here the workmen in *A Midsummer Night's Dream* are discussing their parts in the play they are practising.

QUINCE: Flute you must take Thisbe on you.

FLUTE: What is Thisbe? – a wandering knight.

QUINCE: It is the lady that Pyramus must love.

FLUTE: Nay, faith, let not me play a woman – I have a beard coming.

Poetry and songs appear in some of the plays, with characters singing songs or writing each other poems. Here Ariel in *The Tempest* is singing to Ferdinand.

ARIEL: Full fathom five thy father lies;
Of his bones are coral made;
Those are pearls that were his eyes:
Nothing of him that doth fade,
But doth suffer a sea-change
Into something rich and strange.
Sea-nymphs hourly ring his knell:
Ding-dong.
Hark! now I hear them – Ding-dong, bell.

Shakespeare's poems

Shakespeare didn't just write plays. When plague closed the theatres in 1592–1593, he wrote and published a long poem, *Venus and Adonis*, which made him famous before his plays were well-known. He is also known for his many sonnets. Sonnets are short poems with just 14 lines and a strict pattern of rhymes. Here is the start of his most famous sonnet:

Sonnet 18

Shall I compare thee to a summer's day?
Thou art more lovely and more temperate:
Rough winds do shake the darling buds of May,
And summer's lease hath all too short a date:
Sometime too hot the eye of heaven shines,
And often is his gold complexion dimmed,
And every fair from fair sometime declines...

Shakespeare's words conjure up complex characters with realistic feelings, fears and dreams. This was part of a new direction in drama and has influenced writers ever since.

The Plays

Shakespeare wrote at least 37 plays. They are normally divided into three main types: comedies, histories, and tragedies, as they were in the *First Folio*, the first collection of almost all Shakespeare's plays. It is not known exactly when the plays were written but below are the dates suggested in *The Oxford Shakespeare Complete Works*.

 ## Comedies

In Shakespeare's time, a "comedy" meant a light-hearted story with a happy ending. They are not funny all the way through, but have funny scenes, often using mistaken identities, clever tricks or magic spells gone wrong. They also involve a love story, but have dark and scary bits too!

The Two Gentlemen of Verona	*1589–91*
The Taming of the Shrew	*1590–1*
The Comedy of Errors	*1594*
Love's Labour's Lost	*1594–5*
A Midsummer Night's Dream	*1595*
The Merchant of Venice	*1596–7*
Much Ado About Nothing	*1598–9*
As You Like It	*1599–1600*
The Merry Wives of Windsor	*1599*
Twelfth Night	*1601*
Troilus and Cressida	*1602*
Measure for Measure	*1603–4*
All's Well That Ends Well	*1606–7*
Pericles	*1607*
The Winter's Tale	*1609–10*
Cymbeline	*1610–11*
The Tempest	*1610–11*

 ## Histories

Shakespeare's ten history plays tell the stories of real-life English rulers. He wrote about rulers from the Middle Ages right up to his own Tudor times. However, the history plays are not always very accurate! Shakespeare changed details to suit what he wanted to say or to make the play more exciting.

Henry VI, Part II	*1590–1*
Henry VI, Part III	*1591*
Henry VI, Part I	*1592*
Richard III	*1592–3*
King John	*1596*
Richard II	*1595*
Henry IV, Part I	*1596–7*
Henry IV, Part II	*1597–8*
Henry V	*1599*
Henry VIII	*1613*

Tragedies

Shakespeare's tragedies include some of his greatest plays. The tragedies often focus on a "'tragic hero' – a king or leader who makes a terrible mistake. The plays also feature plenty of battles, murders, ghosts and end in death and disaster. Most of them have funny bits too!

Titus Andronicus	*1592*
Romeo and Juliet	*1595*
Julius Caesar	*1599*
Hamlet	*1600–1*
Othello	*1603–4*
King Lear	*1605–6*
Timon of Athens	*1606*
Macbeth	*1606*
Antony and Cleopatra	*1606*
Coriolanus	*1608*

Lost plays

Writings from Shakespeare's time suggest that he may have written two more plays that we no longer have copies of – *Cardenio* and *Love's Labour's Won*. They might still turn up one day!

Parts of a play

Dramatis personae

Each play begins with a list of all the characters and who they are.

Acts and scenes

Each play has five acts. Each act is split into several scenes. This allows the playwright to change from one setting to another.

Stage directions

Within the dialogue, the playwright gives stage directions: describing who is entering and exiting the stage, what props they have, how they are acting and the background scenery.

Enter stage left with this dagger.

Forsooth! I have forgotten my line!

The actor's sheet

Shakespeare probably only wrote one copy of his plays. This would be used in rehearsal. Each actor would be given his "part", a sheet with his lines and directions. On the night, a cue sheet would be pinned up in the tiring house, and a prompter would keep track of the play and hand out props as the actors went on stage.

Read on to discover more about some of the greatest and best-loved of Shakespeare's works.

A Midsummer Night's Dream

Setting: *A forest near Athens*

This famous, magical comedy is one of Shakespeare's lightest and funniest. The fairies of the wood have made a powerful love potion. When it's put on someone's eyes, they fall in love with the first person they see.

Puck

Four young lovers get tangled up in a web of confusion about who is in love with who, thanks to the fairies messing up their magic.

Hermia and Lysander

The fairy queen, Titania, also falls victim to the magic potion when her husband, Oberon, plays a trick on her.

Titania and Oberon

A FOREST NEAR ATHENS

Meanwhile, a group of workmen try to rehearse a play, to be performed at the wedding of Duke Theseus.

This green plot be our stage...

Flute and Bottom

Lysander, who was in love with Hermia, falls in love with Helena. But Helena is in love with Demetrius.

Titania falls in love with Bottom, one of the workmen, who has been given a donkey's head by the mischievous fairy Puck.

The course of true love never did run smooth.

What angel wakes me from my flowery bed?

Of course, everything gets sorted out in the end, with most of the characters thinking they've dreamed it all. The play ends with a big joint wedding – Hermia to Lysander and Helena to Demetrius – and the workmen's hilarious performance.

Twelfth Night

Setting: *Duke Orsino's palace and the house of the lady Olivia in Illyria*

"If music be the food of love, play on…" This famous opening line, spoken by Duke Orsino, sets the tone for this comedy, which was written to be performed on the last day of the Christmas celebrations. Although its intricate plot includes many funny scenes about what happens when love goes astray, the play has a wintry, melancholic feel.

Duke Orsino is in love with the lady Olivia, but she doesn't return his feelings.

A girl called Viola pretends to be a man called Cesario to get work in Orsino's household.

Orsino and Olivia

Viola falls in love with Orsino, but can't tell him because he thinks she's a man. Olivia falls in love with Viola, also thinking she's a man. It's a very complicated situation!

Meanwhile, Malvolio (Olivia's mean and miserable steward) is tricked by Belch and Aguecheek into thinking Olivia is in love with him. He's a puritan (a strictly religious man) who usually wears black, but he makes a fool of himself by dressing up in yellow stockings and garters! Poor old Malvolio ends up in the madhouse!

Sir Andrew Aguecheek and Sir Toby Belch

Viola, dressed as Cesario

Malvolio

Remember, in Shakespeare's day, the part of Viola would have been played by boy, acting as a girl, pretending to be a man!

As with Shakespeare's comedies, all is sorted out in the end. Orsino marries Viola. Olivia marries Viola's brother, Sebastian. And Malvolio is set free.

Shakespeare is making fun of the puritans, who disapproved of Christmas and the theatre.

Much Ado About Nothing

Setting: *A grand house on the Italian island of Sicily*

There's plenty of mischief and misunderstanding in *Much Ado About Nothing* – one of Shakespeare's funniest and most touching romantic comedies. It's the story of two couples and it still makes us laugh today because people in love have the same fears, hopes and dreams (and make the same mistakes!) as they did in Shakespeare's time.

Benedick, nobody marks you.

My dear Lady Disdain!

Beatrice and Benedick

An excellent wife for Benedick

Leonato and Don Pedro

Take Beatrice and Benedick. They're clever, funny and spend a lot of time together, so why are they always fighting? Because they're head over heels in love, but too scared to reveal their true feelings! So their friends cook up a scheme to bring them together.

Don John and his servant

How canst thou cross this marriage?

Claudio

O God, defend me...

Hero

Evil Don John has also been scheming – to ruin the wedding of Beatrice's cousin, Hero, to the handsome Claudio. Shame and unhappiness drive Hero to fake her own death. But when Don John's wickedness is exposed, she is reunited with her love.

Let's have a dance 'ere we are married.

As the play's title suggests, their worries are a lot of fuss about nothing.

The Tempest

Setting: *An Island*

The Tempest is one of Shakespeare's last four comedies, known as the romances. They often feature older characters, and have a slower pace and more melancholy mood.

The Tempest is about a powerful magician and duke, Prospero, and his daughter, Miranda, who live on a magical island. They were shipwrecked there after Prospero's brother Antonio, with the help of King Alonso, threw them out in order to steal Propsero's dukedom.

Prospero and Miranda

We are such stuff as dreams are made on...

Prospero conjures up a storm (or tempest) to bring everyone back together on the island. This leads to lots of comic mix-ups and a love match between Miranda and Alonso's handsome son, Ferdinand. It also gives Prospero a chance to punish, but also forgive, the wrongdoers, and return everything to its rightful place.

Hark! now I hear them – Ding-dong bell

Ariel

These are not natural events. They strengthen from stranger to stranger.

Antonio, Alonso and Ferdinand

Two strange, non-human characters make the play especially mysterious. Ariel is an "airy spirit" who carries out Prospero's magical commands. Caliban is a dangerous monster, kept captive by Prospero.

Caliban

Richard III

Setting: *England*

This is the story of the power-hungry brother of a king, who plots and murders his way to become King Richard III. Richard is a monstrous villain, yet he is also the play's hero. He is funny and clever, and makes long speeches inviting the audience to feel sorry for him. Shakespeare explores what goes on in the mind of someone who can commit horrific, bloodthirsty acts.

All about power

While they aren't always historically correct, Shakespeare's history plays tell the truth about power. They explore what makes people want power, how they struggle to get it, and what they do with it.

Richard is probably the most evil, power-mad character in all of Shakespeare's works. He declares he will kill anyone who stands in his way.

Richard III also shows how women were often powerless without fathers, husbands or brothers to protect them. After the king dies, Richard closes in on the queen by murdering her male relatives. He forces a noblewoman, Lady Anne, to marry him even though his family killed her first husband.

...thou hateful, withered hag!

The popular image of Richard III, as a crippled, witty and charming, yet mercilessly evil man, comes more from Shakespeare's play than from real history.

Bottled spider... poisonous, bunch-baked toad.

Anne's mother-in-law, Margaret, despises Richard but has no power, so she casts terrible curses on her enemies. Her language is incredibly powerful.

Henry V

Setting: *England and France*

At the other end of the scale is Henry V, a play about a bold medieval king of England and his success in battle against France. Some of the phrases in King Henry's patriotic battle speeches have become a familiar part of the English language.

Once more unto the breach,
dear friends, once more...
...On, on, you noblest English!
...follow your spirit and upon the charge cry
"God for Harry, England and Saint George!"

Stage Battles

Theatres in Shakespeare's time did not use much scenery, and the stage was quite small. They couldn't have lots of soldiers and horses. So, at the start of *Henry V*, a "chorus" or narrator tells the audience that they will have to imagine these scenes.

*"Can this cockpit (theatre) hold the
vasty fields of France?
Oh, pardon! Let us ... on your
imaginary forces work.
Into a thousand parts divide each man.
Think, when we talk of horses,
that you see them!"*

Romeo and Juliet

Setting: *Verona, Italy*

Romeo and Juliet is an unusual tragedy, as it is not about a king or leader, but two teenagers who fall madly in love. Their families are enemies, and a series of fights, mistakes and mix-ups leads to a disastrous ending. The play is still very popular for its realistic portrayal of teenage love, idealism and hot-headed impulsiveness.

In Verona, two rich families, the Montagues and the Capulets, are feuding. But when Romeo Montague and his friends gatecrash a Capulet party in disguise, he falls helplessly in love with Juliet Capulet.

Juliet's parents have plans for her to marry a man named Paris. So Romeo and Juliet quickly marry in secret, helped by Friar Laurence and Juliet's nurse.

Oh Romeo, Romeo!

The Montagues

The Capulets

But another fight breaks out, and Juliet's cousin Tybalt kills Romeo's sparky, funny friend Mercutio. Romeo hastily kills Tybalt in revenge and is banished from Verona.

The friar gives Juliet a potion to make her appear dead, so that she can avoid marrying Paris and Romeo can rescue her. But the message to Romeo goes astray, and he thinks she is really dead. He poisons himself. Juliet awakes, sees what has happened, and stabs herself.

Eyes, look your last! Arms, take your last embrace! And lips... seal with a righteous kiss a dateless bargain to engrossing death!

Julius Caesar

Setting: *Ancient Rome*

Shakespeare wrote several tragedies set in ancient Roman times. Some, such as *Julius Caesar,* are based on real people and events. But despite its title, this tragedy is largely about Caesar's friend Brutus. Caesar is gaining power in Rome, and the people want him to be king. Caesar refuses, but Brutus is still worried that he has too much power. Along with Cassius, Brutus gathers a group of plotters to murder Caesar. The play is best known for this high-drama stabbing scene.

Copying Rome

In Shakespeare's time, people greatly admired ancient Rome, its great empires, buildings and literature. Shakespeare would have grown up reading plays by Roman writers such as Seneca and Plautus, and they had a big influence on him. For example Shakespeare's plays have five acts because he was copying the style of Roman playwrights like Seneca.

Brutus tells the Romans he has done what was best for them, but Caesar's supporter Antony makes a speech that turns the crowd against Brutus. Brutus, haunted by Caesar's ghost, and Cassius both kill themselves after being forced out of Rome.

Et tu, Brute! (meaning "You, too, Brutus?")

Hamlet

Setting: *The Royal Court of Denmark*

Hamlet and the ghost of his dead father

Oh, I am slain!

Ophelia

Polonius

Gertrude and Claudius

Then, venom to thy work.

Hamlet and Laertes

Hamlet is considered by some as Shakespeare's greatest play. It's famous for its in-depth study of Prince Hamlet's state of mind, as he ponders how to avenge his dead father. He pretends to be mad, but is he really going insane? Through a series of botched attempts to do something, Hamlet leads the whole court into a horrific bloodbath.

"To be, or not to be: that is the question." This is one of the most famous of Shakespeare's lines, spoken by Prince Hamlet in turmoil over whether to live or die. His mother, Gertrude, has married his uncle Claudius, who is now on the throne. But Hamlet has seen his father's ghost, who explains that Claudius murdered him.

Hamlet pretends to be insane, so no one suspects him while he plans what to do next. His girlfriend, Ophelia, is upset by his odd behaviour.

Hamlet confronts his mother and accidentally stabs Polonius, Ophelia's father, thinking it is Claudius. Ophelia goes insane with grief and drowns herself.

Ophelia's grieving brother, Laertes, challenges Hamlet to a duel. Claudius prepares a poisoned drink and a poisoned sword to make sure Hamlet is killed. But they get mixed up, and Laertes, Queen Gertrude and Hamlet are all poisoned. Before dying, Hamlet finally stabs Claudius to death.

Hamlet and Claudius

Othello

Setting: *Venice, Italy, and Cyprus*

Othello is the army general of Venice, and a great leader of men. But as a "moor" (north African) he is an outsider in Venice and his secret marriage to Desdemona causes great upset. However, it is a trusted friend that sets about to ruin the marriage, and in turn destroys the young lovers.

Enemy within

Othello's trusted officer Iago is bitter about not being promoted so he convinces Othello that Desdemona has been cheating on him with another officer, Cassio, who is also Iago's enemy.

Iago and Othello

It all hangs on a handkerchief. Iago's wife Emilia is Desdemona's lady-in-waiting. He persuades her to give him Desdemona's handkerchief, and plants it on Cassio, as evidence he has been with Desdemona.

Iago and Emilia

Cassio

Othello

Othello believes Iago. Heartbroken, he swears he'll kill Desdemona. Yet he loves her and struggles with his conscience. He stops himself, then persuades himself, then stops again, willing himself to act. Eventually he smothers her and kills himself.

Yet I'll not shed her blood,
Nor scar that whiter skin of hers than snow...
Yet she must die, else she'll betray more men.
Put out the light, and then put out the light...

Desdemona

Othello learns of Desdemona's innocence and cannot live with the guilt.

Inside the mind

Shakespeare is brilliant at exploring the human mind – how people think, dither and delude themselves on the way to making a decision. He uses long solo speeches, called soliloquies or monologues, to take us inside the troubled minds of his tragic heroes. He shows how the mind can persuade itself of things it wants to believe.

King Lear

Setting: *Ancient Britain*

King Lear tells of an old king of ancient Britain, who is ready to leave his lands and wealth to his three daughters, Goneril, Regan and Cordelia. But his vanity and pride lead him to make a disastrous decision. By the time he learns the true meaning of love and loyalty, it's too late.

King Lear asks his daughters to declare how much they love him. Goneril and Regan make grand speeches, but Cordelia simply speaks the truth – that she loves her father as a daughter should. Furious with her, Lear disowns Cordelia and gives her nothing.

Cordelia leaves for France, where she marries the king.

I cannot heave my heart into my mouth: I love your majesty according to my bond; No more nor less.

Goneril and Regan

Cordelia

Lear

Goneril and Regan, Lear's insincere daughters are richly rewarded – Lear divides the kingdom between them. They then plot against Lear and bully him.

Oh sir, you are old... You should be ruled and led.

Regan and Cornwall blind Gloucester who tries to warn Lear.

Gloucester

Edgar

Edmund

Meanwhile, the Earl of Gloucester is also having problems with his children. His son Edmund tricks him into thinking his other son, Edgar, is plotting to kill him. Like Lear, Gloucester falls for the trick, and treats his most loyal child unfairly.

Gloucester is blinded and Lear goes mad.

By trusting the wrong children, Lear and Gloucester both become pitiful, tragic figures. In the end, almost every character dies, Lear of grief when he hears of Cordelia's death.

Cordelia is executed on return from France.

Blindness

Seeing and blindness are important themes in *King Lear*. Lear and Gloucester are blind to the truth about which of their children are good, and which evil. But Gloucester is literally blinded by Regan's husband, Cornwall – in one of the most horrifying scenes in all of Shakespeare's works.

Macbeth

Setting: *Scotland and England*

Macbeth is a typical example of a tragic Shakespeare hero. Though he begins the play as a good man, thirst for power leads him to commit evil deeds – eventually driving him to madness, despair and a bloodsoaked downfall.

Hail Macbeth, that shalt be king hereafter!

A great war general and cousin of the Scottish king, Macbeth is successful and respected. He meets three witches who make him think he could be even more powerful.

I have done the deed.

Who would have thought the old man to have had so much blood in him?

I have no words. My voice is in my sword.

After being encouraged by his ambitious wife, Macbeth murders King Duncan in order to claim the crown himself. But the guilt and fear of being found out doesn't go away.

Macbeth becomes so troubled it slowly drives him insane. He becomes a lonely, cruel tyrant. Lady Macbeth is also so consumed with guilt that she kills herself.

The play ends with a bloody battle. Macbeth's arch-enemy Macduff tracks him down and destroys him. Malcolm, Duncan's rightful heir, claims the throne.

Shakespeare's Legacy

Today, Shakespeare is known as one of the greatest and most influential writers who ever lived. His works have been translated into over 80 different languages and are still read and performed all around the world.

A wizard says goodbye

Shakespeare is thought to have died on his 52nd birthday. In his last few years as a writer, he worked with other playwrights such as John Fletcher. But the last play he wrote alone was *The Tempest*. At the end of the play, the great wizard Prospero swears he will give up his magic powers, break his magical staff and throw his book of spells into the sea. It's often thought that this was a message from Shakespeare himself, saying it was time for him to retire.

The greatest!

After his death, Shakespeare's friends and fellow writers agreed he was one of the best writers of his age. When the *First Folio* of his works was printed in 1623, it included poems and introductions praising Shakespeare. He was called "the wittiest poet in the world". The great playwright and poet Ben Jonson said, "He was not of an age, but for all time."

"I'll break my staff,
Bury it certain fathoms in the earth,
And deeper than did ever plummet sound,
I'll drown my book."

For all time

Since then, his plays have been performed all over the world and translated into many languages. Composers have borrowed Shakespeare's stories to create great ballets and operas. And with the arrival of film and television, the plays have been reworked with big casts, magical special effects, imaginative scenery and real settings. Over 400 years later, his plays still have meaning for us. Whether he wrote about love or murder, kindness and friendship, or jealousy and revenge, he chose situations and emotions that still ring true today.

"You still shall live,
such virtue hath my pen."

Sonnet 81

Glossary

chamberpots
Large pots in which people used to go to the toilet at night

cobblers
People who mend shoes

delude
To be deceived into believing something that isn't true

dialogue
Lines spoken in a play

duel
A prearranged fight between two people, often to settle a quarrel

feuding
Arguing, fighting or a general ill-feeling between two people or groups

gatecrash
To arrive at a party uninvited

heckling
Interrupting a performer with shouts or jeers

influential
To have the ability or power to affect other people

lead
A heavy, soft metal

legacy
The things left by a person after his or her death

melancholic
Miserable and mournful

metaphor
When a person or thing is described as being something else, for example a timid person is a mouse, or a brave person is a lion

monologue
A long, solo speech

patriotic
Devoted to one's country

pickpocket
A thief who steals from a person's pocket or bag

playwright
A person who writes plays

prompter
Someone who has a script and reminds actors of their lines off-stage

prose
All writing that is not in verse

role
Another name for a part or character in a play

simile
When a person or thing is described as being like something else

smithies
A metal workshop

soliloquies
Long, solo speeches

tanneries
A place where animal skins are turned into leather

thronged
Gathered together in a crowd

troupes
Groups of theatrical performers

Further information

www.shakespeareforschools.com

A dedicated website linked to this book and offering further information about Shakespeare's life, characters, language and plays.

Shakespeare Birthplace Trust
www.shakespeare.org.uk 01789 204016

This charity owns and maintains the five houses associated with Shakespeare in Stratford-upon-Avon.

Shakespeare's Globe
www.shakespearesglobe.com
020 7902 1400 *(enquiries)* 020 7401 9919 *(box office)*

Carefully reconstructed near the original site of Shakespeare's Globe, this is the closest you can get to reliving what is was like to see a play in Shakespeare's day.

The Royal Shakespeare Company
www.rsc.org.uk 0844 800 1110

The RSC is one of the most famous theatre companies in the world, based at the Royal Shakespeare Theatre in Stratford-upon-Avon.

Shakespeare 4 Kidz
www.shakespeare4kidz.com 01883 723444

The UK's National Shakespeare Company for children and young people, performing child-friendly musical adaptations of Shakespeare's plays.

Index

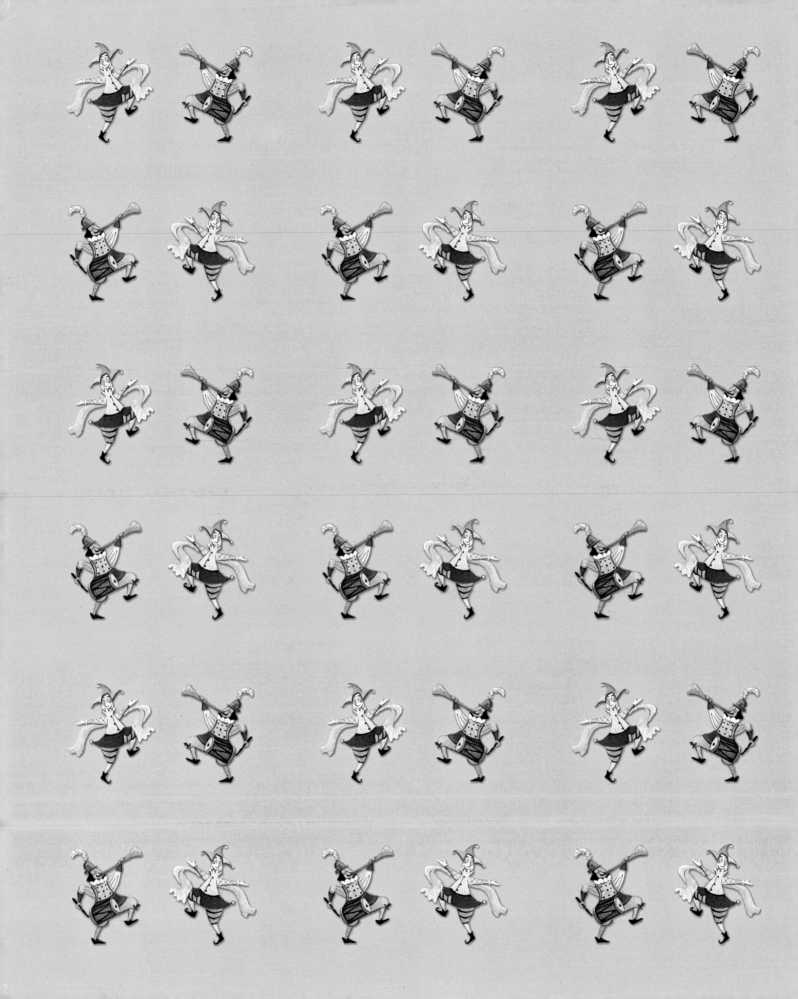